ISBN-13: 978-0615793634
ISBN-10: 0615793630

www.nuancepress.com

FOREWORD

Several years ago
Several severed ears ago
Several surreal summers gone
I died, but just went on and on...

This is the first significant collection of my poetry I've been able to not only assemble but actually publish and distribute through the amazing mechanisms of the wondrous-beyond-belief Internet, an incredibly sophisticated system of tubes, apparently (Ha! Whod'a thunk it?) most cleverly arrayed and arranged in such a fiendishly complicated and diabolically inscrutable manner so as to insure that no creature of man and woman born may gaze upon the terrible beauty therein, without being transfixed and rapidly absorbed into a new world of amazing high-resolution happy pixelated never-ending waiting.

Seems like a lifetime ago, when I first started down the Tubular Way. Fraught with many dangers, it is... and as many other captured souls can certainly attest, after years have elapsed, unnoticed, the unfortunate long-lost Pilgrim eventually finds, to their distress, that they have been changed, remade... transformed into something they no longer recognize.

Normal light no longer feels natural; the old realities no longer apply, and life beyond the Pod begins to seem less and less genuine and three-dimensional.

But through the magic of the Many Tubes That Are One, in time we come to realize that we too are tubes, amazing and inexplicable; we see how some tubes suck, and some tubes blow; and some tubes illuminate, and some darken; they darken the heart, and the soul, and even the underwear, impartially... yet we see too that all these weird and wiggly and wanking tubes are forever joined together in a big ugly hopeless knot... and we rejoice at this knowledge.

Now we can never be alone. Now we are *all* piano-playing cats.

Which, when you think about it, beats the hell out of being powerless, clueless members of America's secret slave caste, the mid-to-lower classes.

This is the behemoth that now embraces us entire, and we respond to its endless purrs and pulsations the way people always do, because how can ya turn down a vibrating bed, especially if you live in Hell? Yep, this is the New Deity of Brilliant, Blinding, Endless Tubage we are all caught up within at this time...

And I for one am so glad for this, because I have always had this absolute revulsion for editors everywhere. I hate 'em. True, I haven't known that many. But I've known a few, and they were ALL soul-searingly EVIL.

Really. Nasty little Smeagols, every one of 'em.

So all Praise the Giant Flying Spaghetti Monster that is the Internet! Praise its Mighty Tubes! Who needs editors anymore? All they do is *suck time.*

Decades of precious time. Right from your bones.

Fuck you, editors of the world. FUCK YOU.

Oh, and just in case they're still at all valid, I'd like to also praise and humbly thank God and/or Gumby–whichever is the True Big Dude Standin' Above It All, And Quite Probably Wankin' It... cuz who really knows, anyway? Not me. I just want to make sure I pay the proper respects here.

Cuz it's taken me most of a rather misbegotten and insanely difficult existence to finally get my work out there for all of you to perhaps look at and go "Hmmm..."

That would be pretty neat. If some of you do that.

Incidentally, many of these poems were made the old-fashioned way, with real corn syrup and lots o' love!

I do hope, sophisticated reader, that you will truly enjoy this heapin' helpin' from my admittedly-bizarre bean.

(Freakin' eggheads. Readin' POETRY! Seriously?
Pitiful.)

D X Stone
Apr 1, 2013

Van Gogh's Ear

D X Stone

Nuance Press

Good Deal!

There is a universe within your inner ear
And in THAT universe, another inner ear
And in THAT inner ear, ANOTHER universe
And in THAT universe, a tiny little purse
Made from a sow's ear's innards, and inside of THAT:
A universe, a toothbrush AND a smart new hat!

Missing Molecule

Somewhere in a box
That used to house a tiny jewel
There's a tiny little missing molecule
A molecule, in fact, that has been missing
Since before the very first beginning
Of this magic universe, eternal-cursed...

The molecule itself is fine–
Everything *else* is out of line...

The missing molecule!
It's missing from a cuticle!
The missing molecule!
It's marvelous! It's beautiful!

Its missing is mysterious
It tends to give one pause
It's quite profound and serious
It flies against all laws

It shouldn't be, but there it is
(And where it is ain't where it was!)
We couldn't see it if it was
Becuz becuz becuz becuz
Becuz becuz becuz becuz becuz...

(Which now explains, of course, how
Fuzzy Wuzzy Wuzzy really wasn't...
And why ol' Uncle Buzz is cussin' –
Even though we *know* he doesn't!)

Car Loan Blues

Fill in your name–your street address
If you don't know just take a guess
Fill in the numbers that you're known by
Fill in the hours that have gone by
Since the time that you were born
Fill in the form

Fill in the hours yet remaining
Indicate special interests and training
Tell us about every job you have done
Give us a list of awards you have won
Write a short essay on your deepest fears
Give us the exact dimensions of your ears
Fill in the number of times you've said 'thanks'
Fill in the blanks
Fill in the blanks

Tell us exactly how much you were paid
This will account for four-fifths of your grade
Answer the questions about masturbation
And about your favorite radio station
Of course this is all privileged information
Write it in pen–do it again!
Write it in pen–do it again!

Fill in the intimate details of
Your very first fistfight and very first love
Write a report on all things that you do
Fill out three copies–the first is for you
The second's for us and the third is destroyed
Fill in the void
Fill in the void

Give an account of each time you have cried
Tell us about every instance you lied
Delineate any deviant notions
And estimate the precise weight of emotions
Then multiply this by ninety-nine nines
Then multiply this by ninety-nine nines
Then multiply this by ninety-nine nines
Then multiply this by ninety-nine nines
Fill in the lines

The Boy With The Prehensile Tail

The boy with the prehensile tail
He oughta be tossed right in jail
Or driven out upon a rail
The boy with the prehensile tail

He learned to hide it in his youth
Who could be trusted with the truth
To deal with the enormity
Of his bizarre deformity

He tied it up between his thighs
To hide it well from prying eyes
And walked a little strange but otherwise
Appeared like all the other guys

The boy with the prehensile tail
He oughta be tossed right in jail
Or driven out upon a rail
The boy with the prehensile tail

And no evaluation
Of his unique mutation
Could supply a reason
For this genetic treason

It hurt a lot to sit on it
He never could find pants to fit
And he would be the first one to admit
How much he wanted to get rid of it!

The boy with the prehensile tail
He oughta be tossed right in jail
Or driven out upon a rail
The boy with the prehensile tail

And then one day some normal folks
Learned about this clever hoax
And they agreed for his own sake
To burn the odd boy at the stake

They found his strange appendage
Utterly repelling
Which proves the truth–the tale's in the telling
And now the tail has ended

The boy with the prehensile tail
He oughta be tossed right in jail
Or driven out upon a rail
The boy with the prehensile tail

Potato Bugs
(Mr. Potatohead's Lament)

Potato bugs
Run up and down my rugs
Fill up the bowls and mugs
They're nature's little thugs

Potato bugs
They fill the stairs and halls
Rolled up in little balls
Can't even see the walls

Potato bugs
Always annoying me
Hugging and cloying me
They really seem to be enjoying me

Potato bugs
They're friggin' everywhere!
And I just wouldn't care
Except they're in my ears and nose and hair

Potato bugs
They live inside my head
That's what the doctor said
I wish that I was dead
Potato bugs

Jonathan Fell

Jonathan fell!
He fell through clouds–he fell through space
Jonathan fell!
He fell like a pro–he led with his face

Jonathan fell!
He dropped like a stone–he dropped like a rock
Jonathan fell!
He fell and he fell and he just couldn't stop

Jonathan fell!
He fell past a system of strange sideways sewers
Jonathan fell!
He fell past a butcher, a baker, some brewers

Jonathan fell! Jonathan fell!
He died and he's dead and he went straight to hell
He wasn't a bad guy–he was kinda nice
Maybe they'll give him some ice

Jonathan fell!
He fell through a landscape of death and decay
Jonathan fell!
He didn't say nothin'–he had nothin' to say

Jonathan fell!
He fell past strange doorways engraved with odd numbers
Jonathan fell!
He fell through a grove of huge floating cucumbers

Jonathan fell! Jonathan fell!
Gravity grabbed him and tossed him pell-mell
He was here just a moment ago–now he's gone
Who's gonna water his lawn?

Jonathan fell
He fell through an ocean and into a hole
Jonathan fell
And that's the last anyone's seen of his soul

Jonathan fell! Jonathan fell!
Maybe he's better off–maybe he's swell
Maybe he's fat now and laughing alot
Maybe–but then maybe not

Not a Paranoid

I'm not a paranoid, I'm not
Not a paranoid, I'm not, I'm not
I know people have it out for me
Even people in my family

Cuz everyone's out to getta me
They all say that they're not and that I'm nuts
I know everyone's my enemy
Everybody hates my guts

Second verse
Worse than the first

I'm not a paranoid, I'm not
Not a paranoid, I'm not, I'm not
I know people plot behind my back
Someday soon I'm sure that they'll attack

'Cuz everyone's out to getta me
They all would love to see me lose my head
Wish I was someone else instead'a me
Everybody wants me dead

Let's Get Redundant

Let's get recumbent
C'mon, get down on da flo'
Like a right-wing pundit
Let's see how low we can go
Let's get redundant
Let's do it mo' and then mo'
Let's do it hundits
Of times in a row

Let's get redundant
Let's get redundant
Let's get redundant
Let's get redundant
Let's get redundant
Let's get redundant
Let's get redundant
Let's get redundant
Let's get redundant
Let's get redundant
Let's get redundant
Let's get redundant
Let's get redundant
Let's get redundant

Let's just keep beatin' it
To no real end
Let's keep repeatin' it
Again and again
C'mon, let's do it
Til it's 'WAY overdone
Let's do it to it
Til it just ain't no fun

Let's get redundant
Let's get redundant
Let's get redundant
Let's get redundant
Let's get redundant
Let's get redundant
Let's get redundant
Let's get redundant
Let's get redundant
Let's get redundant
Let's get redundant
Let's get redundant
Let's get redundant
Let's get redundant
Let's get redundant

Let's get redundant
Let's get redundant
Let's get redundant
Let's get redundant
Let's get redundant
Let's get redundant
Let's get redundant
Let's get redundant
Let's get redundant
Let's get redundant
Let's get redundant
Let's get redundant
Let's get redundant
Let's get redundant
Let's get redundant
Let's get redundant
Let's get redundant
Let's get redundant
Let's get redundant
Let's get redundant
Let's get redundant
Let's get redundant

Sleeping Dogs

Let sleeping dogs lie
Let lying dogs sleep
Let lambs lie down with lions
Let wolves lie down with sheep

Let everything that crawls lie down
With everything that creeps
And then let's see if anything
At all gets any sleep

Let all the smothering rules be damned
Let bygones be bygone
Let dogs and lions, wolves and lambs
Lie down upon your lawn

Let gravity in stairways
Go upside down, then out
Let all dogs go their own way
Each to his own snout

Let dogs be gods and gods be dogs
Let all dogs be themselves
Let pupdogs lie with pollywogs
Let Elvis lie with elves

What a Show!

The Age is split in two
And no one knows just what to do
Or where to go
Nobody knows just how to feel
Or how to deal
Or what to say and do to heal

The hole within our world
The shard within our hearts
It's gone beyond our wildest fears
It may just be beyond our arts
To heal this wound, so deep, so grave
It may just be too late to save
Us from the fires
Of our desires...

But what a show!
For all the universe to witness
When we go!
We'll light up like a Christmas tree
And everyone who sees will know that

We Were Here
That we were full of fire and heat and beer
That we were fueled, quite foolishly
By beer and fear and fire
And we took the whole thing pretty high
And then we took it even higher...

Like Icarus,
If we had one fatal flaw
Then this was it:
We were blinded by the lovely light we lived in
And we never really knew just when to quit

The Vowel & Consonant War Song

The vowels and the consonants
Couldn't get along
Cuz' the more versatile vowels
Saw the consonants as wrong

They really couldn't see just what
The consonants were for
So the vowels and the consonants
Went to war

The vowels were outnumbered
(Though no numbers were involved)
So they sent spies behind the lines
To get this problem solved

They tried to get the W
To split off to their side
And they lobbied for the X as well
Though it could not decide

Then they stopped to double-cross a T
Cuz' it was on their route
And they nearly got stung by a B
While getting the L out

But the consonants weren't worried
They just sat around all day
And made some T and watched TV
And smoked a bunch of J's

Cuz' even though they'd lost their I's
Of course they still could C
And the vowels soon surrendered
Cuz' they had to take a P

The vowels signed an IOU
As penance for their views
They promised that from that day forth
They'd watch their P's and Q's

Y of all was wisest
It was neutral all along
And that's the
Vowel and Consonant War Song

Stupid Duckhead

My friend kept the head of a duck in a jar
And he set the thing up on the dash of his car
And he tried to pick girls up
Yeah he tried to pick girls up
But he really didn't get too far

It's that duckhead, I said
See, I took him aside
And I told him that duckhead
Was ruining his ride

It's that duckhead, you nut
I tried telling the fool
It's a nice duckhead but
It smells pretty uncool

That duckhead's unlucky
I gently persuaded
That's one unlucky ducky
Whose head should be hated!

You should think this through twice
It's a duckhead! It's dead!
Don't you think fuzzy dice
Might be nicer instead?

I told him ten times but he just wouldn't listen
He was stubborn and stupid–a man with a mission
He thought it impressive, he thought it unique
And sometimes he'd pick it right up by the beak
And wave it around like a king or a prince
And the smell was enough to make fishermen wince
Til I tired of it all–I just stopped taking his calls
And I haven't seen him since...

But I heard...yes I heard...

'Bout that one fateful day
He tried taking a curve much too fast...

(look out look out LOOK OUT LOOK OUT!–
ScreeeeeecchCRASH!)

And when they finally pulled him
From the twisted, smoking wreck
(wouldn't ya just know it)
He had that stupid duckhead
Shoved right up his ass

And that's what they put on his stone in the ground
And it's been there ten years and a half
And people still come from miles around
Just to read, and think, and laugh

It's that duckhead, I said
See, I took him aside
And I told him that duckhead
Was ruining his ride

But he just wouldn't listen
He just didn't hear
And he died with a duckhead
Stuck up his rear

And he never got there
No he never got lucky...
'Less you count his affair
With the head of a ducky

WANTED

WANTED:

Blind albino wino
      w/a tiny spined vagina
Nasty
      into rhinoplasty
Likes to please
      diseased and ghastly
Clothing optional
      and lastly
Into intravenous drugs
      and buggering big ugly bugs

For long walks in acid rain
      w/deranged poet

      thoroughly insane

Manic-Depressive

I'm manic-depressive
Compulsive-obsessive
I'm passive-aggressive
And I couldn't care less if
They cut up my brain
Cuz I know I'm insane
And I'm always in pain
And I can't stand the strain cuz
I'm manic-depressive
Compulsive-obsessive
I'm passive-aggressive
And I couldn't care less if
They cut up my brain
Cuz I know I'm insane
And I'm always in pain
And I can't stand the strain cuz
I'm manic-depressive
Compulsive-obsessive
I'm passive-aggressive
And I couldn't care less if
They cut up my brain
Cuz I know I'm insane
And I'm always in pain
And I can't stand the strain cuz
I'm manic-depressive...

Karl's Killer Collar

Karl's killer collar
Cost his tightwad Boss a glossy dollar
It was way too tight!
And the color–Blechh!
And it choked him 'til it broke his neck!
The Boss's funny money shoes
Were lost, so he had naught to lose
Someone, it seemed, had crossed him twice!
Had tossed him like a pair of dice!
Two shoes amiss!–it wasn't fair
It wasn't nice! It got him pissed!
Re-fried his rice!
Got his dander up!
Turned his ass to ice...

He blew a fuse and screwed the pooch
He drank a fifth of filthy hooch
And he went right out to find a device
To kill Karl dead!
To kill Karl twice!
Cuz' last week he'd just fired
A fella name of Fred
Fred had made him feel afraid
So afraid that he had fled
Without even so much as a hat on his head!

But the Boss, he returned with a posse!
He returned with a judge and a jury!
He returned full of fudge and a fiery fury!
With one insane desire, one obsessive need;
To see this Fred fired! To watch this Fred bleed!
For this Fred was no friend
To the Boss in the end–
He was false! Just a liar
Who deserved to be fired!
Thought the Boss with a smile
Like a long metal file...

And when the Boss indeed returned
Fred wasn't only fired–
He was set afire and burned!
And his flesh was then eaten
My sources have learned
Save his head, heart and holes
And the soles of his feet
And a few other leftovers nobody eats...

Poor Fred was finally freed
He died and now he's dead
The Boss has finally lost
His foolish fear of Fred, and Karl as well

Now that they've gone to the other side
To hide in Hell

And Carol cried and cried
For Karl and Fred, now dead
Had died for Carol's sins
(Or so it's said)
Both of them brought down to earth
To herald in the birthing of
An awesome gilded age!
That was simply not to be...
Poor Carol's in a gilded cage
The Boss says
"Nothing in this life is free!"

And the very thought of birthing?
It hurts the Boss's brain
His children fill him with a chilling rage
Again and yet again...
He turns and hurls himself on Carol carelessly
And airlessly they grapple like a pair of feral beasts
Trying both to bite the apple cursed–
To bite the apple first–
To bite that goddamn apple
Once at least

Some Possible Alternatives

Why can't we all just get along?
Why do we always get it wrong?
Why can't we all just sing a song?
Or bang a gong?
How 'bout we all just gang a bong?

A Prayer

Lord, I am your monster...
Do whatever you want.

You were going to anyway.

Meanwhile, At A Nice Intimate Fluptud
In The Year One Zillion

The pretty hippopotapuss
Spoke to the well-scranked splatopod:
"Perhaps all gluds are sub-gorns
To some wunkered hunkering Wilbur-God."

"I wish that I could talk to It a bit,"
She mused, "In prentless proot."
"I'd like to scraw your scrumbled bronklemux,"
He tried, "And truff your snoot."

Van Gogh's Ear

When Vincent sent his sheared-off ear
Off to the maid
What did it hear, I wonder,
When she opened up the morning mail?...
A scream? A sigh? A moaning wail?
Softly whispered words of love's devotion?
Did she hold it to her own ear
To hear the ocean's roar?
And, hearing, seem to see bright stars
That spun and shined
Within the artist's spinning shining half-mad mind?

Did she wrinkle up her nose and poke it with a probe?
Or nibble at its little lobe?
Did she disrobe and spend a carnal hour or so–
Just her and it
Alone within her room–
Holding it so close that it could hear
The ocean's roar within her womb?

Did she hold it up and shout into it,
"NO NO NO!"
Or "Testing! Testing! One! Two! Three!"
Or "Echo!... echo... echo..."

Perhaps she took it for a piece of jewelry
(Earliest art deco)
Thought it quite endearing
Hung it from her own ear as an earring
So it could always hear whatever she was hearing...
Whispered words of love
From other paramours, mouthed soft and tender–
Or did she simply ship it back Return to Sender?

This tragic bit of flesh
Detached perforce from magic mind
And yearning still to find a single sympathetic note
Within the sad and sorry song
Of his long and lean and lonely time...
Here the ear, perhaps, that heard her best
The night she laughed right in his face
And told him he was daft, confessed
She found him totally bereft of charm or grace...

What need for such extremity extreme?
A little listening enemy?
He'd need that like he'd need
Another hole within his head...
Kill the treacherous messenger! Indeed! Yes!
Kill the traitor dead!...

And turn his one good ear away
Quit listening at all...
Turn his lonely countenance into a stony wall instead
Fill up the hole with alcohol
Or luminescent light
Or lead...

He died halfway that day
Lost half his face and half his sense
Erased in anguish deep, immense...
A sacrifice of half his lonely life
For longing for the other half he couldn't have...
A love... a wife...

He shouldn't have.
He shouldn't have been forced to make that choice...
He'd already lost half his voice
Half his passion
Half his sight...
And when he finally sacrificed the other half
The world lost such a rare
And special light...

I hope that when she opened it
It did not have to hear her laugh again...

The Blonde Leading the Blind

If the blind were leading the blind I bet
That most would get out of the woods, and yet
If it were a blonde that were leading the blind
They'd *never* get out, 'less they left 'er behind!

The Lil' People

The lil' people always wanna
Purchase lil' pieces of each other
The lil' people keep their
Lil' secrets in a secret lil' cupboard

The lil' people always want their
Surfaces to be kept neat and shiny
And if they want a lil' raise at work
Then they just kiss a lil' heiny

Some like to tackle things
Much larger than themselves
But most would rather
Tickle something tiny
They stick their knick-knacks up
On lil' metal shelves
Lots of them have voices
High and whiny

The lil' people like to go to
Teeny tiny lil green machines
And take out lots and lots of money
And go buy a new appliance

And every lil' person is indebted
To the credit companies
That loom above their heads like
Monumental luminary giants

And lots of lil' people are
 At least a lil' crazy
And lots of them work very hard
Cuz someone called them lazy
Yes someone called them useless
As a riding mower to a moose!
And what can lil' people do
To deal with such immense abuse?

And here's a lil-known and lil-noted lil' people fact
A lil' bit of insight into how most lil' people act:

The lil' people won't admit it to themselves
When they make a silly lil' blunder
The lil' people are like magic lil' elves
Without the magic or the wonder

And only lil' people know
Where all the lil' people go
When trouble rears its ugly mug
They're tickling a ladybug...

The lil' people really want
Assurances of guaranteed insurance
Or else they feel like tiny lil' fishes
Tossed about in random currents

They don't cooperate cuz they would
Rather leave each other in the lurch
And if their guilt is great than they can
Go and get berated in a church

The lil' people like to pay their
Share of taxes right on time
Some make so lil' money that it
Doesn't cost them half a dime

But some of them make more than
Lots of lil' people ever even dream
And it's funny cuz the biggest lil' people
Do not have to pay a thing

It's usually the lil' things
That make most lil' people mad
But big things are beyond most lil' people
And that's just too bad

Cuz they can't organize and so
They live the teeny lives of slaves
And slave away both night and day
Til they go to their tiny lil' graves

But one day legends say
That lil' people everywhere will rise
And on that fateful day
That lil' people come together to decide
That they have heard enough
Of all the bigger lil' people's bullshit lies
I fear we're gonna see
A real lotta lil' people suicides...

I Troid

I troid to tell you how AAAAK! feel
But we're both unk-employed
And so KURK! cell-phttt choices
Turned out Hiss! than choice and now
We're KAHL!ways BLARguing, all-KURG! annoyed
And every third--erk--fourth word's lost
Within the void
I troid to tell you how KAAAA! really felt
I really troid

And sometimes EBERT every UGGGER!
Motherferk-fin' word KISS! lost
I cannot KILL!culate the tragic cost
It's simply SKERZLL!!
So I guess we're truly SHNOST!!

Cuz when our whole vocabulary's
Trimmed down to SKREETT and KRICK!
It's hard to tell if you're GOK! is SURRR-FREET!!
Or if someone's just being a dick

Keepin' Bees

I think I'm gonna start keepin' bees
Why the heck shouldn't I?
I think I'm gonna start keepin' bees
Give me one good reason why
I'll keep any old darn bugs I please
I need no alibi–I need no alibi

There's not much muss and fuss with keepin' bees
It don't cost much to start a hive
They'll never break your heart or steal your keys
And take your Beamer for a drive
It does a body good to keep some bees
It keeps your heart alive
It keeps your heart alive

Well, I been givin' it quite a bit of thought
Maybe more than anyone really ought
Cuz I'm kinda 'fraid 'a them little guys
They got them com-pound eyes

But I find myself strangely attracted to that
Incessant buzzing noise they make
And I really like the fact that they won't
Steal my car, y'know?

And they're always zippin' around
Makin' free honey...
It's kinda funny

(no it isn't!!!)

Some people like to climb up mountainsides
Some are lonesome cowboy types
Some will pressure you to view their slides
Some try to sell you handy wipes
And there are those who like amusement rides
And guys who play bagpipes
And guys who play bagpipes

But I am not like any one of these
(I couldn't wear those bagpipe clothes!)
I'd cross a hundred seas to keep some bees
It's just my karma, I suppose
There's nothin' quite as fun as keepin' bees
'Cept when they sting your face
'Cept when they sting your face!

Smokin' Song

Smokin' dope'll never getcha
Into trouble 'less they catcha
Some maryjane'll keep yer brain
In better health, I wanna betcha
It's not a bit immoral, no
It's wholesome and nutritious
And the fact that it's illegal
Only makes it all the more delicious
And at the very worst you'll only
Slow your life a little
Yeah, you may never get around
To masterin' that fiddle
But smokin' dope'll never get ya
In a mad or murderous mood
It's not like drinkin'–you'll just think a lot
And eat a lotta food
It's not like coke or crack or glue
Or heroin or speed
But any idiot would know
That those are nothin' no one needs
And you will never see a buncha
Day-glo snakes a'flyin' atcha
Cuz smokin' dope'll never getcha
Into trouble 'less they catcha

D X Stone

Snortin' crank and doin' crack
Can make ya croak and that's a fact
But no one ever took a toke
And dropped dead of a heart attack
And you won't crash your car on grass
If you follow what I'm sayin'
At worst you might run out of gas
More likely you'll just stay in

Smokin' dope'll never getcha
Into trouble 'less they catcha
The worstest part is worryin'
The DEA is gonna snatcha
But boo won't make you want to steal
To support your habit
And it won't make you want to kill
A little baby bunny rabbit
You'll laugh a little louder
And a little bit more often
You'll smoke too many cigarettes
And do a lotta coughin'
But you won't ever hurt yourself
Or others with a spoon
You'll probably just sit around
And watch cartoons all afternoon
Or spend a lil too much time
Just talkin' to your pets
But that's about as scary as a
Mari-juana madman gets
No you will never see a buncha
Day-glo snakes a'flyin' atcha
Cuz smokin' dope'll never getcha
Into trouble 'less they catcha

Never Alone

You're never alone
Said the clone to himself
You can never go home
Said the orc to the elf

You can never relax
Said the fear to the man
You can't know all the facts
You can't know where you stand

You can't hide—be assured
Said the all-seeing seer
There's no word goes unheard
By my all-hearing ear

You will never be freed
You will never know ease
Said the soil to the seed
Not intending to tease

You will never get out
Said the tingling fear
To the lingering doubt
Spinning webs in the inner ear

Whether

I went to the mountain to talk to the Man
'Cuz I'd heard that his word
Was the Word from Above
I went 'cuz I wanted to learn all I can
And this cat was the Buddha!
A dude o' pure love!

So I went to the peak and I saw this old dude
He was takin' a leak–he was totally nude
So I waited to speak 'cuz I dared not intrude
I'm just not that rude

He led me into a chilly old cave
And he sat in a lotus and beckoned to me
He told me that his name was Dave
And he asked what I wanted and offered me tea

So I sat on a mat and I questioned the cat
I had all kindsa questions 'bout this and 'bout that
And this dude had the answers–he had 'em down pat
I was sure about that

So many questions I had in my head
Buzzin' around like a hatful'a bees...

Whether life is meaningful
Whether love is true
Whether truth is lovely
Whether red is blue
Whether light's a wave
Or just a little dot
Whether it's worth asking
Whether it is not
Whether man's immortal
Or if he's not instead
Whether there's a porthole
In Dan Quayle's head
Whether everything began
With a bang or with a pop
How that argument began
Whether it will ever stop
Whether God's a monster
Coming soon to get us
Whether ham is best with cheese
Or perhaps with lettuce
Whether man will ever learn
Whether there is hope
Whether we will ever turn
Our parents on to dope

I wanted the lowdown, the facts, the straight poop
So many questions I spewed to the dude
And I knew that this guru could give me the scoop
Sitting there on his rock in his cave in the nude

And when I was finished he leaned into me
And he paused, yes he paused, so dramatically
And his olden lips trembled, and then finally
He whispered to me:

"You carry your own weather in your head...
GET YOUR SHIT TOGETHER!"
–that's all the old man said

The Great Hillbilly Spellin' Bee

At the Great Hillbilly Spellin' Bee
No one could even spell "HILLBILLY"
Except for lucky ol' Billy Hill...
He *always* wins!
He always will

Holy Toledo

I wanna go to Toledo
I wanna go there to stay
Holy holy Toledo
I wanna go there today
I wanna live in Toledo
Until the day that I die
I really hear that it's neato
And that's the main reason why

If I could go to Toledo
I'd kiss the ground and I'd cry
And then I'd put up my feet, oh
I'd put 'em up high

They say it's not just a city
They say it's somethin' you feel
They tell me it's really pretty
They tell me it's pretty real

They got jabaka jacuzzi
They got those fuzzy dice ways
They got bald eagles and uzis
And one of these days

I'm gonna go to Toledo
And make my peace with the gods
And I could live in Toledo
Whatever the odds
I'm gonna go to Toledo
Where the people are free
Holy holy Toledo
It's the city for me

They got the best in Toledo
They got the fuzziest dice
Even mosqitoes
In Toledo are nice

They got good food in Toledo
The trees have eatable leaves
They make a big ol' burrito
Ya gotta see to believe

And all the girls don't wear panties
In Toledo, I'm told
They blow away Cincinnati
Where all the panties have holes

That's why I'm goin' to Toledo
For the food and the girls
There's no place else like Toledo
No place else in the world
That's why I'm goin' to Toledo
So don't you get in my way
Holy holy Toledo
Famed city of Hay

But could I live in Toledo?
Could I ever fit in?
Would I be stopped at the border?
Would I *ever* get in?

I could catch up on my knittin'
And I could collate some notes
Or I could practice my spittin'
Or wrestle some goats

Cuz they got sports in Toledo
That no one else does
Like "Shootin' the Hairball"
Or "Chewin' the Fuzz"

That's why I'm going to Toledo
Because of all that I've heard
I'm goin' like a torpedo
I'm flyin' straight as a bird
Cuz when I think of Toledo
I just cannot be down
Holy holy Toledo
It's my kinda town

Y'know I'm comin' from Cleveland
And I'm headin' due west
Cleveland's ok but I'm leavin'
Cuz Toledo's the best

They walk around in pajamas
They don't dress for the day
They don't peel their bananas
They've found a *better* way

And everyone in Toledo
Tells the same saucy joke
Concerning famous Judge Ito
And a pig in a poke

That's why I'm goin' to Toledo
To hear that joke bein' told
I wanna hear it complete-o
I hear it never gets old
That's why I'm goin' to Toledo
Besides, the ride's not too long
Holy holy Toledo
I'm already gone

To A Real Mother

M is for the millions that she wasted

O speaks only of her orange glow

T is for the terror that we tasted

H is for the hell she brought in tow

R is for her breath of radiation

A is for her anger, don't you know?

Put them all together, they spell Mothra

The Monster Who Ate Tokyo

Someday

One day, some day, we'll all awake
And somehow know just what it takes
To make the whole world right once more
And we'll all run right out the door
To shout the news out loud and clear
For everyone everywhere to hear...
And we'll all shout in perfect sync
Billions of souls, a single link
A chorusing of reason clear
That fills the whole world's atmosphere
A vision shared, pristine and pure
A knowledge new to man, and sure

And on that day the doves will soar
There'll be no suffering anymore
And everyone will sing and shout
And on that day, or thereabout
There'll be an end to war and spite
And everything will be alright
There'll be an end to lies and greed
And finally we'll all be freed
There'll be an end to hate and fear
There'll be an end to death...
But until that day
I wouldn't hold my breath

www.ingramcontent.com/pod-product-compliance
Lightning Source LLC
Chambersburg PA
CBHW071733020426
42331CB00008B/2017